From the movie

DISNEY
FROZEN

Ages 6–7

Disney LEARNING

Reading and Comprehension

LEARNING WORKBOOK

Scholastic Children's Books
Euston House,
24 Eversholt Street,
London NW1 1DB, UK

A division of Scholastic Ltd

London • New York • Toronto • Sydney • Auckland
Mexico City • New Delhi • Hong Kong

This book was first published in Australia in 2014 by Scholastic Australia.

Published in the UK by Scholastic Ltd, 2015

ISBN 978 1 4071 6283 6

Printed in United Kingdom by Bell and Bain Ltd, Glasgow

4 6 8 10 9 7 5

Welcome to the Disney Learning Programme!

Children learn best when they are having fun! The **Disney Learning Workbooks** are an engaging way for your child to develop their reading and comprehension skills along with fun characters from the wonderful world of Disney.

The **Disney Learning Workbooks** are carefully levelled to present new challenges to developing learners. Designed to support the National Curriculum for English at Key Stage 1, they offer your child the opportunity to practise skills learned at school and to consolidate their learning in a relaxed home setting with support from you. With interactive stickers, puppets and easy-to-read mini-books, your child will have fun reading and understanding all sorts of stories.

Confident readers understand, remember and talk about what they read. They use a variety of strategies to make sense of what they are reading, such asking and answering questions, noting important details, predicting what might happen next and making connections with their own experiences. This **Disney Learning Workbook** will help your child practise these comprehension strategies.

Throughout this book you will find 'Let's Read' stories featuring characters from the movie **_Frozen_** for you to enjoy sharing with your child. Reading for pleasure and enjoying books together is a fundamental part of learning. Keep sessions fun and short. Your child may wish to work independently on some of the activities or you may enjoy doing them together – either way is fine.

Have fun with the Disney Learning programme!

Developed in conjunction with Catherine Baker, Educational Consultant

Let's Read and Understand

In this book, you will find lots of fiction and non-fiction texts. You will be asked to find details that will help you learn who is in the story, where the story is taking place and what the main idea of the story might be. By answering these questions you'll start to understand stories better and become a stronger reader.

As you read a story, think about what might happen next. Look for clues and then make a prediction. Read on to see if it happens.

Try retelling a story to help you remember what happens. After you read, stop and think about what took place in the beginning, middle and end of the story.

Look at how the information in a non-fiction text is written. Does it inform, explain or discuss the topic?

_____

Talk about the books you've read with your friends! What surprised you? What made you laugh? What new things did you learn?

_____

Don't forget to use what you know to think about what you are reading. **This helps you understand what you are reading.**

Information books are called non-fiction. Stories are called fiction.

It is a quiet day in Arendelle. Princess Anna wanders around the halls of the royal castle, looking for something to do. There are many beautiful paintings on the walls. Anna has seen them all before. Today, she wants to do something new.

'I'm bored!' she says to her sister, Elsa. 'There's nothing new to do around here.'

Elsa looks at her little sister. Anna is always looking for fun things to do outdoors. But maybe she doesn't know that there are lots of fun things to do indoors as well.

'Why don't you try reading a book?' Elsa suggests. 'The castle library is filled with so many great books. I'm sure we can find one you'll like.'

Anna laughs. 'I don't know why I didn't think of that,' she says.

Elsa smiles. 'Let's go to the library. We will find the perfect story for you.'

Snowballs

Anna and Elsa are in the castle. Elsa has made it snow inside! They are having a snowball fight. It is great fun. Olaf comes into the castle.

'Hello, friends!' he says. 'What are you doing?'

Anna grins. 'We are having a snowball fight,' she says. 'I am winning!'

Elsa giggles. 'I wouldn't be so sure about that!' She grabs three snowballs and throws them at her sister. Olaf catches one of them.

'Hey!' he says. 'I have a snowball now, too. Can I join in?'

Let's Understand

Read the questions about the story *Snowballs*.
Put a ✔ next to the correct answer.

1. **What are Anna and Elsa doing?**

   ☐ cleaning the castle

   ☐ building snowmen

   ☐ having a snowball fight

2. **How many snowballs does Elsa throw at Anna?**

   ☐ one

   ☐ two

   ☐ three

3. **What do you think will happen next?**

   ☐ Olaf will join in the game.

   ☐ The sun will come out.

   ☐ Anna will eat an apple.

Let's Think About Characters and Setting

Think about the characters and setting in the story **Snowballs**.
Answer the questions by drawing a picture in each box.
Label the pictures.

Who are the characters?

Where does the story take place?

Let's Write

Draw a picture of yourself having fun in the snow.
Write a sentence that goes with your picture.

Let's Learn
Word Meanings

Read the question. Write the word from the box that answers the question. Find the matching stickers.

| grabs | grins | giggles |

1. What word from the story means <u>smiles</u>?

   _____

   -

   _____

2. What word from the story means <u>laughs</u>?

   _____

   -

   _____

3. What word from the story means <u>takes</u>?

   _____

   -

   _____

Let's Review
Characters and Settings

Read the story, then answer the questions.

Sven and Olaf

Sven and Olaf went flying in hot-air balloons. They were high up in the air.

'Can you see the mountains over there, Sven?' Olaf asked. Sven nodded.

'I can see the castle over here!' said Olaf.

The friends had fun on their big adventure.

1. Circle the character names in the story above.

2. Draw a line under the place where the story takes place.

3. What can Sven and Olaf see from the balloon?

Sven can see _____.

Olaf can see _____.

4. What things can you see around you?

I can see _____.

This is a piece of non-fiction.

Horses

Horses have four legs. They eat plants like grass and can run very fast.

People have worked with horses for many years. We can ride horses. They can also pull carts and wagons. They are very useful animals.

Horses live on farms and also in the wild. Groups of horses are called herds.

Let's Write

Write a sentence about something you know about horses.
Draw a picture to show what you know.

Read the story, then answer the questions.

Sven Can Skate!

Sven is at the frozen lake. It's time to skate. Oh, no! Sven does not know how to skate! Sven is sad.

'I'll teach you,' says Olaf. They go to the lake. 'Put your feet on the ice,' says Olaf. 'Now, push them forwards slowly.'

Sven tries to skate all day. He slips and slides everywhere. At last, he glides over the ice. Olaf glides next to him. 'Sven, you can skate!' Olaf cries.

Oh dear! Sven and Olaf glide right into a pile of snow!

'Now let's learn how to stop!' Olaf says. The friends laugh together.

Let's Understand

Read the questions about the story *Sven Can Skate!*
Put a ✔ next to the correct answer.

---

1. Where is Sven?

☐ at school

☐ at the lake

☐ at a friend's house

---

2. How does Sven feel at first?

☐ excited

☐ happy

☐ upset

---

3. Why do Sven and Olaf laugh at the end of the story?

☐ Sven can skate, but he can't stop.

☐ Olaf makes a joke.

☐ It's time for lunch.

Let's Learn About
Story Structure

Write what happens at the beginning,
middle and end of *Sven Can Skate!*

Beginning

_____

Sven cannot _____ .

⬇

Middle

_____

Olaf _____ him how to skate.

⬇

End

_____

Sven finally _____ on the ice.

Let's Write

Draw a picture of yourself doing something fun.
Write a sentence that goes with your picture.

Let's Learn About Opposites

Some words have **opposite** meanings.
Happy and sad are **opposites**.
Use a word from the box to write the **opposite** word.
Find the matching stickers.

under	cold	night

1. hot

_____
- - - - - - - - - - - - - - - - - -
_____

2. over

_____
- - - - - - - - - - - - - - - - - -
_____

3. day

_____
- - - - - - - - - - - - - - - - - -
_____

Let's Retell the Story

Carefully cut out the pictures on the dotted pink lines.
Fold along the blue lines so the pictures will stand up.
Use the pictures to retell **Sven Can Skate!**

Be careful of sharp
scissors. Ask an
adult to help.

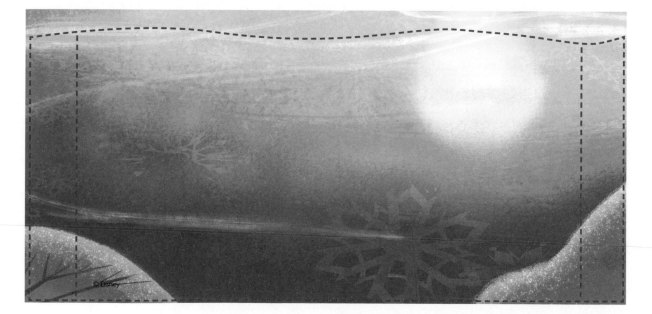

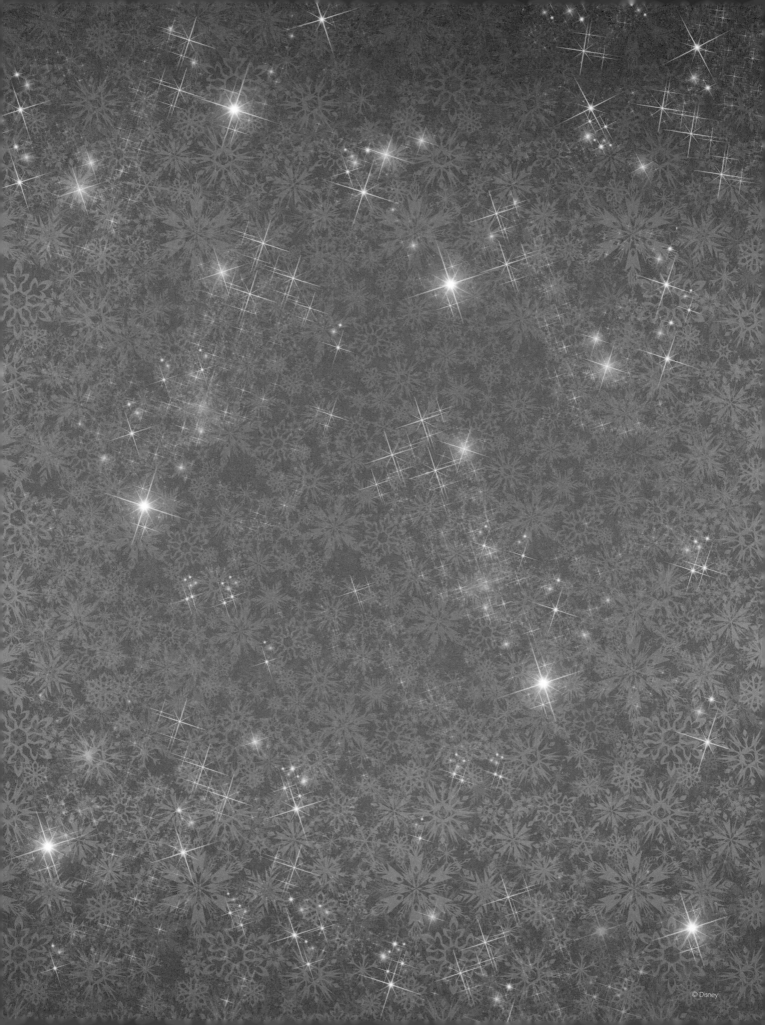

Let's Write

Write a sentence about yourself learning something new.
Draw a picture of what happened.

_____

- -

_____

_____

- -

_____

Read the story, then answer the questions.

A New Reindeer Friend

Anna, Elsa and Olaf went up to the snowy mountains for a picnic. They saw a baby reindeer. He was stuck on a cliff!

'I can help!' said Elsa. She made a ramp out of ice. 'Climb up the ramp,' she told the reindeer. But the reindeer slipped on the ice and could not climb it.

'I can help!' said Anna. She slid down the ramp holding some rope. She tied the rope around the reindeer. 'Pull him up,' she told Elsa and Olaf.

Soon the baby reindeer was safe and sound with his new friends!

Let's Understand

Read the questions about *A New Reindeer Friend*.
Put a ✔ next to the correct answer.

---

1. Where did Anna and Elsa go?

- ☐ to the shops
- ☐ to the moon
- ☐ to the mountains

---

2. What did they find?

- ☐ a baby reindeer
- ☐ a snowman
- ☐ biscuits

---

3. Who pulled the reindeer to safety?

- ☐ Anna
- ☐ Elsa and Olaf
- ☐ Sven

Let's Learn About Story Sequence

Find the stickers for *A New Reindeer Friend*.
Put them in the right order.
Use the stickers to retell the story.

Beginning

Middle

End

Let's Write

Write a sentence about making new friends.
Draw a picture that shows you making new friends.

Let's Learn Words with the Same Meaning

Some words mean the same thing.
Big and large mean the same thing.
Use a word from the box to write words with the same meaning.
Find the matching stickers.

afraid   glad   angry

1. **mad**

_____

- - - - - - - - - - - - - - - - - - -

_____

2. **scared**

_____

- - - - - - - - - - - - - - - - - - -

_____

3. **happy**

_____

- - - - - - - - - - - - - - - - - - -

_____

Let's Make Predictions

Anna is going to read a book called **Boats**.

What do you think **Boats** will be about?

_____

- -

_____

Put a ✔ next to two things you might learn about in **Boats**.

☐ Boats travel on land.

☐ Big boats are called ships.

☐ Some ships have sails.

☐ Sails are made from plastic.

Now, let's read to find out!

This is a piece of non-fiction.

Boats

Boats help people to travel across water. There are lots of different boats. Very big boats are called ships. People have travelled in ships for many years.

Ships can have big sails. They are big sheets of stiff cloth. When the wind blows, it pushes the sails. This moves the ship forward.

The front of a ship is called the prow. Sometimes the prow can look like a person or an animal. The back of a ship is called the stern. A ship's flag is flown from the stern.

Let's Learn About Diagrams

A ship is made of many parts.
Look at the diagram.

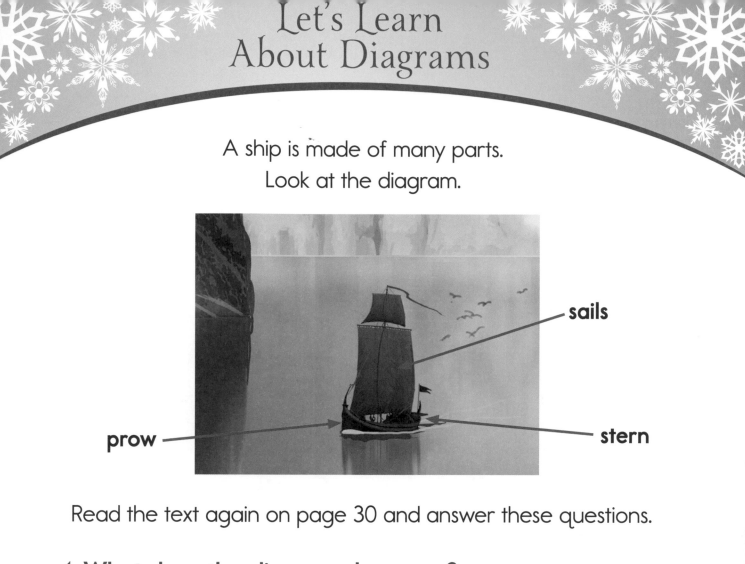

Read the text again on page 30 and answer these questions.

1. What does the diagram show you?

_____

- -

_____

2. Where is the ship's flag?

_____

- -

_____

3. What pushes the sails?

_____

- -

_____

Read this non-fiction text, then answer the questions.

Kronborg Castle

Kronborg Castle is in Denmark. It is a very big castle. It is also very old.

Kronborg Castle was built by King Eric of Denmark in the year 1420. That is about 600 years ago! The castle is built out of stone. It was built on an island between Denmark and Sweden. There was a big fire at the castle 200 years after it was built. King Christian of Denmark fixed the parts of the castle that had burned. The castle has a high wall all around it, many towers and a big courtyard in the middle.

Many kings lived at Kronborg Castle over hundreds of years. Today, it is a museum. People come to see the beautiful castle and all the treasures inside.

Only an act of true love will thaw a freezing heart

ELSA

Anna

Elsa

Let's Understand

Read the questions about **Kronborg Castle**.
Put a ✔ next to the correct answer.

1. **Kronborg Castle is _____.**

   ☐ very old

   ☐ make-believe

   ☐ very new

2. **The castle is built out of _____.**

   ☐ cake and chips

   ☐ stone

   ☐ bricks

3. **The castle was once damaged by _____.**

   ☐ an earthquake

   ☐ a storm

   ☐ a fire

4. **Today, Kronborg Castle is _____.**

   ☐ a museum

   ☐ where the King of Denmark lives

   ☐ no longer standing

Let's Understand

Read about **Kronborg Castle** again.
Complete the sentences.
Draw a picture to go with each sentence.

The castle has many _____ .

There is a high _____ around the castle.

Let's Write

Draw a picture of a real or pretend castle you would like to visit. Write a sentence about your picture.

Let's Review Words

Draw a line to match words that are **opposites**.

hot	day
sad	cold
over	happy
night	under

Draw a line to match words that have the same meaning.

afraid	angry
mad	scared
glad	chilly
cold	happy

Let's Look at Cause and Effect

Cause and effect are about what happens to a character because of what they have done. Read this story about Olaf.

The Bees and the Coconut

Olaf was on holiday. He sat under a big coconut tree. He saw a big, shiny coconut high up in the tree.

'I want to pick that coconut for Queen Elsa.' He climbed up the tree trunk. He twisted the coconut and it came off the tree. Then he heard a buzzing noise. It was coming from the coconut!

'Oh dear!' said Olaf. 'It is not a coconut. It is a beehive!' The bees came out of the hive. They flew around Olaf's head. They sat on his nose.

'It's lucky I'm not afraid of bees,' Olaf said. 'They can't sting my carrot nose. But I will put the hive back into the tree. I can find another coconut to give to Queen Elsa!'

What was the cause? What did Olaf do?

_____

- -

_____

What was the effect? What happened?

_____

- -

_____

Let's Write

Draw a picture of something you are afraid of.
Write a sentence that goes with your picture.

ANNA'S ICY ADVENTURE

Anna met Sven and Kristoff on a cold night.

She was looking for her sister.

Anna found her sister Elsa.

She lived in a pretty ice castle!

Sven and Kristoff helped Anna.

They travelled across the snow.

The snow was pretty.

They met a snowman.

His name was Olaf.

Happy Marshmallow

Marshmallow is feeling grumpy. Olaf is going to cheer him up!

First, Olaf throws a snowball at Marshmallow. Marshmallow is surprised! He plays tag with Olaf.

It is time to go home. Marshmallow and Olaf skate down the frozen river back to the castle. They are just in time for hot chocolate!

Write 1, 2, 3, 4 to show the order of these events.

_____ They drink hot chocolate.

_____ Olaf throws a snowball.

_____ It is time to go home.

_____ Marshmallow and Olaf play tag.

Let's Read

Read this piece of non-fiction about the northern lights.

The Northern Lights

When you look up at the night sky, it is dark apart from any stars. But if you went to the North Pole, you might see lots of colours in the sky! These are called the northern lights.

There is a blanket of air around the Earth called the atmosphere. Light from the Sun bounces off the blanket of air. The light changes the colour of the night sky. The northern lights look like waves of blue and green. They are brightest from December to March.

If you went to the South Pole, you would see the southern lights. They are also waves of blue and green light. They are brightest from May to October.

The northern and southern lights are also called the *Aurorae*. They are like our planet's very own fireworks!

Let's Understand

Read the questions about *The Northern Lights*.
Put a ✔ next to the correct answer.

1. **Why do the northern lights happen?**

   ☐ We set off fireworks.

   ☐ Light bounces off the atmosphere.

   ☐ Nobody knows.

2. **When are the northern lights most bright?**

   ☐ May to June

   ☐ August

   ☐ December to March

3. **When are the southern lights most bright?**

   ☐ May to October

   ☐ December to March

   ☐ April

4. **What colour are the northern and southern lights?**

   ☐ red and gold

   ☐ blue and green

   ☐ silver

Let's Compare and Contrast

Use the words in the box to complete the sentences about the northern and southern lights. Read how the lights are the same. Write how the lights are different.

North   December   South
May   October   March

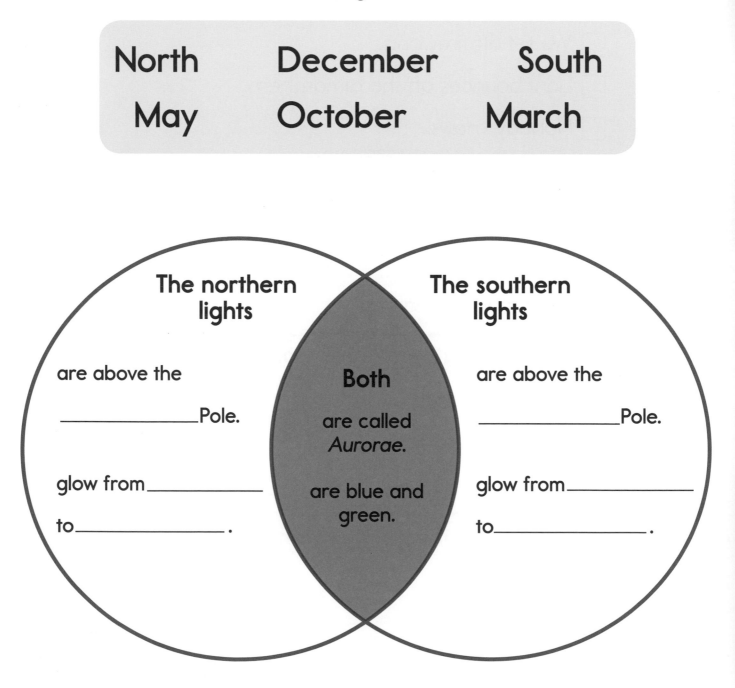

The northern lights

are above the

_____Pole.

glow from_____

to_____ .

Both

are called *Aurorae.*

are blue and green.

The southern lights

are above the

_____Pole.

glow from_____

to_____ .

Let's Compare

The northern lights glow thousands of metres up
in the sky. That's much taller than we are!
How tall are you? Ask a friend to measure you.

I am _____ centimetres tall.

Draw something that is taller than you.
Draw something that is shorter than you.
Label your pictures.

Taller than me	Shorter than me

Let's Learn
Compound Words

Some words are made with two words.
Words that are made with two words are **compound words**.

Butterfly is a **compound** word.

butter + fly = butterfly

Write the **compound** words.
Find the matching stickers.

sun + shine

_____

- -

_____

snow + man

_____

- -

_____

lamp + post

_____

- -

_____

bed + room

_____

- -

_____

Sisters

Anna and Elsa are sisters.

Elsa likes to be neat.
Anna likes to be messy.

Anna likes playing outdoors.
Elsa likes reading indoors.

But Anna and Elsa both like to make snowmen!

Think about Anna and Elsa.
Write how they are alike and how they are different.

Anna likes	They both like	Elsa likes

This is a play about Anna and Elsa when they were little. Choose to be either Elsa or Anna.

Do You Want to Build a Snowman?

Characters:

Elsa   Anna

Elsa: It's time for bed, Anna.

Anna: I can't sleep. Let's do something fun!

Elsa: What would you like to do?

Anna: Do you want to build a snowman?

Elsa: (laughs) All right! (Elsa waves her hand. It begins to snow.)

Anna: First, we need to make a big, round body.

Elsa: Now we're going to need a head.

Anna: We can use these twigs for arms!

Elsa: And these rocks make good eyes. Hmm. Something is missing.

Anna: (claps) I know! He needs a big, carroty nose!

Elsa: (laughs) Yes! That is just what he needs, Anna!

Let's Retell the Story

Cut out the puppets. Tape each puppet to a spoon.
Use the puppets to retell **Do You Want to Build a Snowman?**
Make your voice sound like the characters in the play.

© Disney

© Disney   © Disney   © Disney

Let's Write

Write something that Anna and Elsa might say to each other.

Read the story, then answer the questions.

A Birthday Mystery

Anna was excited about Kristoff's birthday party. Elsa had made Kristoff an ice model! It sparkled in the sun.

Anna had baked a cake. 'It's your favourite!' she told Kristoff. Everyone went to eat cake and other yummy birthday food.

Later, it was time for Kristoff to open his birthday presents. Sven gave him a carrot. Olaf picked him a bunch of flowers. Next, Elsa went to give Kristoff his ice model. But it was nowhere to be found!

Where did the model go? Everyone looked high and low.

'I can't find it,' said Olaf. 'All I see is this puddle of water.'

'Of course!' said Kristoff. 'The sun was shining through the window. The model must have melted!'

Elsa waved her hand and made another beautiful model!
'Happy birthday, Kristoff!' everyone said.

Let's Understand

Read the questions about *A Birthday Mystery*.
Put a ✔ next to the correct answer.

1. What did Anna make for Kristoff?

☐ a cake

☐ an ice model

☐ a card

2. What went missing from the party?

☐ three cupcakes

☐ a hat

☐ an ice model

3. What clue did Olaf see?

☐ crumbs

☐ a puddle

☐ footprints

4. What happened to the missing thing?

☐ It melted in the sun.

☐ It was stolen.

☐ It went for a walk.

Let's Learn About Problems and Solutions

Read the story **A Birthday Mystery** again.
What happens to the ice model? What is the problem?

_____

- -

_____

- -

_____

- -

_____

- -

How does Elsa solve the problem? What is the solution?

_____

- -

_____

- -

Let's Write

Draw a picture of something you lost.
Complete the sentences.

I looked _____ .

I found my _____ .

Let's Learn
Word Meanings

Read each sentence.
Write a word from the box that has the same meaning.
Find the matching sticker.

| race | fun | jump | pretty |

1. This word means *very nice to look at.*

   _____

   -

   _____

2. This word means *to run very fast.*

   _____

   -

   _____

3. This word means *to have a good time.*

   _____

   -

   _____

4. This word means *to spring into the air.*

   _____

   -

   _____

Let's Review
Problems and Solutions

The Great Idea

Read the story, then answer the questions.

Olaf loved the summertime. He loved to sit on the beach and play in the park. But Olaf was a snowman. A snowman could not stay out in the sun. He would melt if he got too warm!

Elsa had a great idea. She made a small, cold cloud above Olaf's head. It would keep him cool when the day got warm.

Olaf was so happy. He could now spend time in the sunshine!

Put a next to the correct answer.

1. What is Olaf's problem?

☐ He liked the beach.

☐ He would melt if he got too hot.

☐ He didn't do his homework.

---

2. How did Elsa solve the problem?

☐ She created a cold cloud.

☐ She gave Olaf some ice.

☐ She took Olaf to the mountains.

Read the poem,
then answer
the questions.

Summertime

You know, winter is fun
But when it's all done
Out comes the sun!
It's time for summer.

Birds sweetly sing
And they flutter their wings.
Want to play on the swings?
Come on, it's summer!

It feels so grand
To lie on the sand
With a cool drink in my hand
In the summer.

When the warm breeze blows
The grass quivers and grows.
It tickles my nose
Every summer!

Oh, summer is great!
Every year I can't wait.
I'm counting the dates
Until summer!

Let's Read the Poem Again

Read the poem again following the instructions below.
Mark off each instruction with a ✔ when you're finished.

☐ **Make your voice excited when you see !**

☐ **Make your voice go up when you see ?**

☐ **Read the poem fast.**

☐ **Read the poem slow.**

☐ **Read the poem taking turns with a friend.**

You read one line.
Your friend reads the next line.

☐ **Use spoons to keep a beat.**

Hit two spoons together as you read.
Tap out the rhythm in the poem.

Let's Write

Help write a story about two sisters.
One sister is called Elsa.
Write the name of the other sister.

There is a reindeer in the story.
What colour is the reindeer?

Write the reindeer's name.

Now ask an adult to help you cut out the next page.
Fold it to make a book. Fill in the blanks where you see them.
Colour the pictures.

Who Lives on the Mountain?

Who lives on the north mountain? Elsa and her sister, _____, are going to find out.

4 1

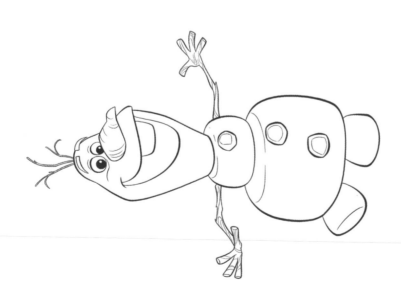

They reach the top of the mountain. It is not scary at all! No big snow monster lives on the mountain. A friendly snowman lives there instead.

'Hi!' says the snowman. 'I'm Olaf. I like warm hugs.'

They all go back down the mountain.

4

Kristoff and his reindeer, _____
go with the sisters. They will help them on
the trip. The reindeer's fur is warm and
_____ .

'I heard that a scary snow monster lives on the
mountain,' says Kristoff. 'He is big and covered in
sharp ice. You can hear him roar when the wind
blows.'

Elsa and _____ shiver. 'I hope you
are wrong,' says Elsa.

Anna looks at Elsa.

'You love to read, don't you, Elsa?' she says. 'When you were little, you loved to be inside with a good book.'

Elsa smiles. 'And you were always much happier on your pony outside!'

'Even though we are sisters, we are so different,' says Anna.

'Yes,' says Elsa. 'But we have lots of things in common. Now you love to read, too!'

'That's true!' cries Anna. 'I love the stories I have read today. I can't wait to share them with my friends.'

'Let's go and find them,' suggests Elsa. 'I think I saw them playing in the snow outside.'

Anna is excited. 'Good idea, Elsa!' she says.

The sisters go outside to find Olaf, Sven and Kristoff. They are playing outside in the snow.

'Hi, Kristoff!' Anna calls. 'Hi, Olaf! Hi, Sven!' She waves to her friends. They come over to say hello.

'What have you two been doing today?' asks Kristoff.

'We have been in the castle library,' says Elsa. 'Anna and I have been reading some wonderful stories.'

Olaf gasps. 'I just *love* stories!' he says. 'I love them nearly as much as I love the sunshine and the summertime!' Sven nods his head. He loves stories, too.

Elsa laughs. 'Well, then, you're going to love what Anna has planned! She has brought lots of stories to share with all of us.'

Everyone is excited. What a perfect way to end a perfect day!

Answers

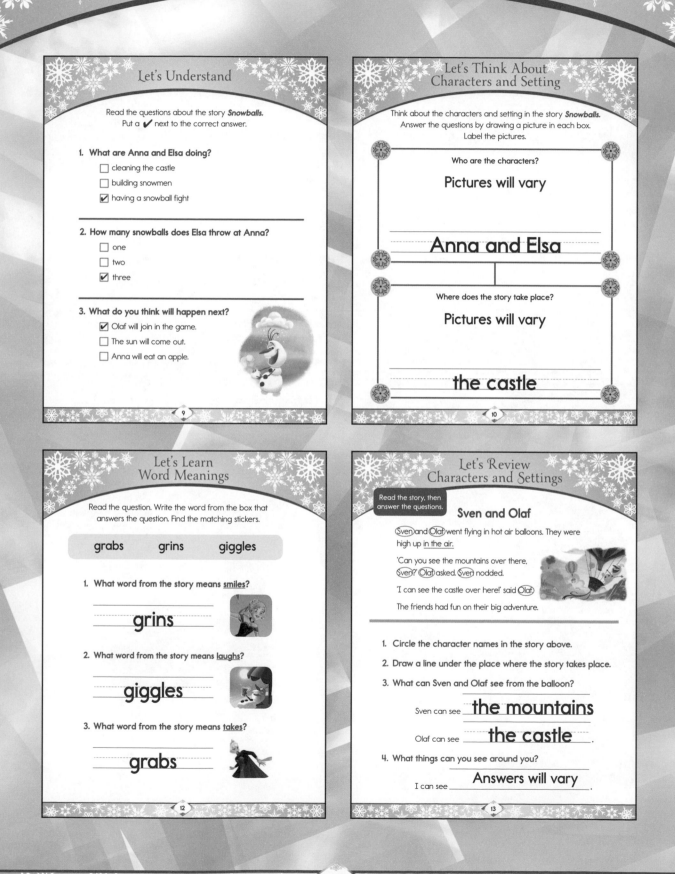

Let's Understand

Read the questions about the story *Snowballs.*
Put a ✔ next to the correct answer.

1. What are Anna and Elsa doing?
   - ☐ cleaning the castle
   - ☐ building snowmen
   - ☑ having a snowball fight

2. How many snowballs does Elsa throw at Anna?
   - ☐ one
   - ☐ two
   - ☑ three

3. What do you think will happen next?
   - ☑ Olaf will join in the game.
   - ☐ The sun will come out.
   - ☐ Anna will eat an apple.

9

Let's Think About Characters and Setting

Think about the characters and setting in the story *Snowballs.*
Answer the questions by drawing a picture in each box.
Label the pictures.

Who are the characters?

Pictures will vary

Anna and Elsa

Where does the story take place?

Pictures will vary

the castle

10

Let's Learn Word Meanings

Read the question. Write the word from the box that
answers the question. Find the matching stickers.

| grabs | grins | giggles |

1. What word from the story means <u>smiles</u>?

   grins

2. What word from the story means <u>laughs</u>?

   giggles

3. What word from the story means <u>takes</u>?

   grabs

12

Let's Review Characters and Settings

Read the story, then answer the questions.

Sven and Olaf

(Sven) and (Olaf) went flying in hot air balloons. They were
high up <u>in the air.</u>

'Can you see the mountains over there,
(Sven)?' (Olaf) asked. (Sven) nodded.

'I can see the castle over here!' said (Olaf).

The friends had fun on their big adventure.

1. Circle the character names in the story above.

2. Draw a line under the place where the story takes place.

3. What can Sven and Olaf see from the balloon?

   Sven can see **the mountains**

   Olaf can see **the castle**.

4. What things can you see around you?

   I can see **Answers will vary**.

13

66

Answers

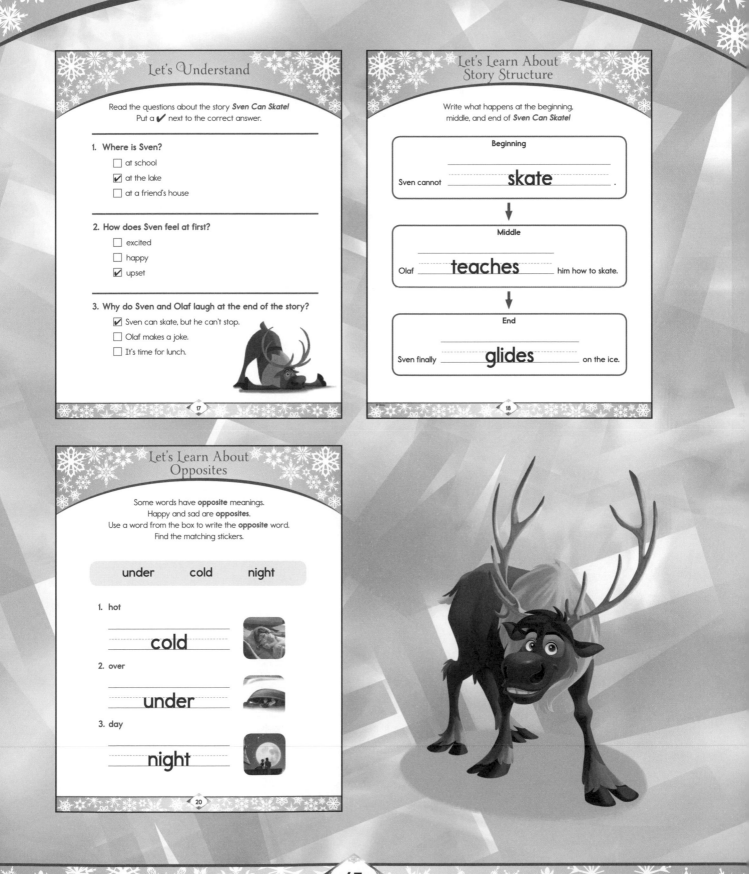

Let's Understand

Read the questions about the story *Sven Can Skate!*
Put a ✔ next to the correct answer.

1. **Where is Sven?**
   - ☐ at school
   - ☑ at the lake
   - ☐ at a friend's house

2. **How does Sven feel at first?**
   - ☐ excited
   - ☐ happy
   - ☑ upset

3. **Why do Sven and Olaf laugh at the end of the story?**
   - ☑ Sven can skate, but he can't stop.
   - ☐ Olaf makes a joke.
   - ☐ It's time for lunch.

17

Let's Learn About Story Structure

Write what happens at the beginning,
middle, and end of *Sven Can Skate!*

Beginning

Sven cannot _____ **skate** _____ .

↓

Middle

Olaf _____ **teaches** _____ him how to skate.

↓

End

Sven finally _____ **glides** _____ on the ice.

18

Let's Learn About Opposites

Some words have **opposite** meanings.
Happy and sad are **opposites**.
Use a word from the box to write the **opposite** word.
Find the matching stickers.

under	cold	night

1. hot

   _____ **cold** _____

2. over

   _____ **under** _____

3. day

   _____ **night** _____

20

Answers

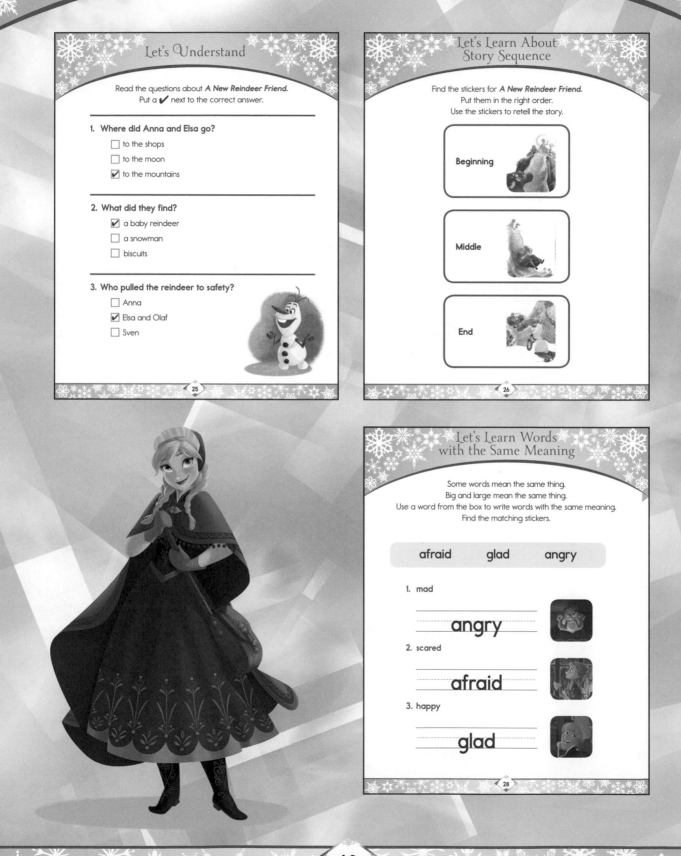

Let's Understand

Read the questions about *A New Reindeer Friend*.
Put a ✔ next to the correct answer.

1. **Where did Anna and Elsa go?**
   ☐ to the shops
   ☐ to the moon
   ☑ to the mountains

2. **What did they find?**
   ☑ a baby reindeer
   ☐ a snowman
   ☐ biscuits

3. **Who pulled the reindeer to safety?**
   ☐ Anna
   ☑ Elsa and Olaf
   ☐ Sven

25

Let's Learn About Story Sequence

Find the stickers for *A New Reindeer Friend*.
Put them in the right order.
Use the stickers to retell the story.

Beginning

Middle

End

26

Let's Learn Words with the Same Meaning

Some words mean the same thing.
Big and large mean the same thing.
Use a word from the box to write words with the same meaning.
Find the matching stickers.

afraid   glad   angry

1. mad
   angry

2. scared
   afraid

3. happy
   glad

28

Answers

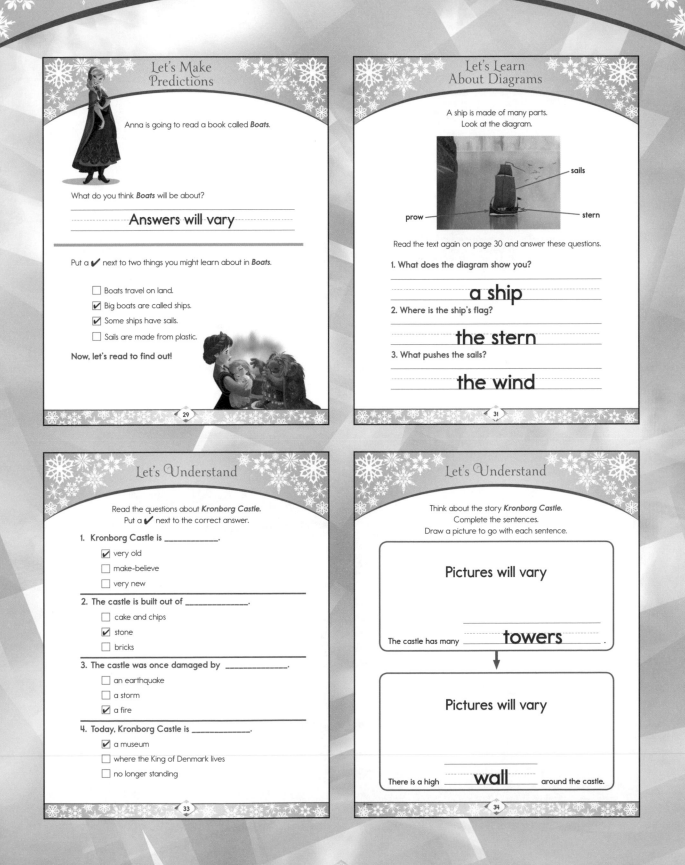

Let's Make Predictions

Anna is going to read a book called *Boats*.

What do you think *Boats* will be about?

Answers will vary

Put a ✔ next to two things you might learn about in *Boats*.

☐ Boats travel on land.
☑ Big boats are called ships.
☑ Some ships have sails.
☐ Sails are made from plastic.

Now, let's read to find out!

29

Let's Learn About Diagrams

A ship is made of many parts.
Look at the diagram.

sails

prow

stern

Read the text again on page 30 and answer these questions.

1. What does the diagram show you?

a ship

2. Where is the ship's flag?

the stern

3. What pushes the sails?

the wind

31

Let's Understand

Read the questions about *Kronborg Castle*.
Put a ✔ next to the correct answer.

1. Kronborg Castle is _____.
   ☑ very old
   ☐ make-believe
   ☐ very new

2. The castle is built out of _____.
   ☐ cake and chips
   ☑ stone
   ☐ bricks

3. The castle was once damaged by _____.
   ☐ an earthquake
   ☐ a storm
   ☑ a fire

4. Today, Kronborg Castle is _____.
   ☑ a museum
   ☐ where the King of Denmark lives
   ☐ no longer standing

33

Let's Understand

Think about the story *Kronborg Castle*.
Complete the sentences.
Draw a picture to go with each sentence.

Pictures will vary

The castle has many **towers**.

Pictures will vary

There is a high **wall** around the castle.

34

Answers

Let's Review Words

Draw a line to match words that are **opposites**.

hot — cold
sad — happy
over — under
night — day

Draw a line to match words that have the same meaning.

afraid — scared
mad — angry
glad — happy
cold — chilly

36

Let's Look at Cause and Effect

Cause and effect are about what happens to a character because of what they have done. Read this story about Olaf.

The Bees and the Coconut

Olaf was on holiday. He sat under a big coconut tree. He saw a big, shiny coconut high up in the tree.

'I want to pick that coconut for Queen Elsa.' He climbed up the tree trunk. He twisted the coconut and it came off the tree. Then he heard a buzzing noise. It was coming from the coconut!

'Oh dear!' said Olaf. 'It is not a coconut. It is a beehive!' The bees came out of the hive. They flew around Olaf's head. They sat on his nose.

'It's lucky I'm not afraid of bees,' Olaf said. 'They can't sting my carrot nose. But I will put the hive back into the tree. I can find another coconut to give to Queen Elsa!'

What was the cause? What did Olaf do?

He picked a coconut.

What was the effect? What happened?

It was a beehive.

37

Answers

Let's Review
Cause and Effect

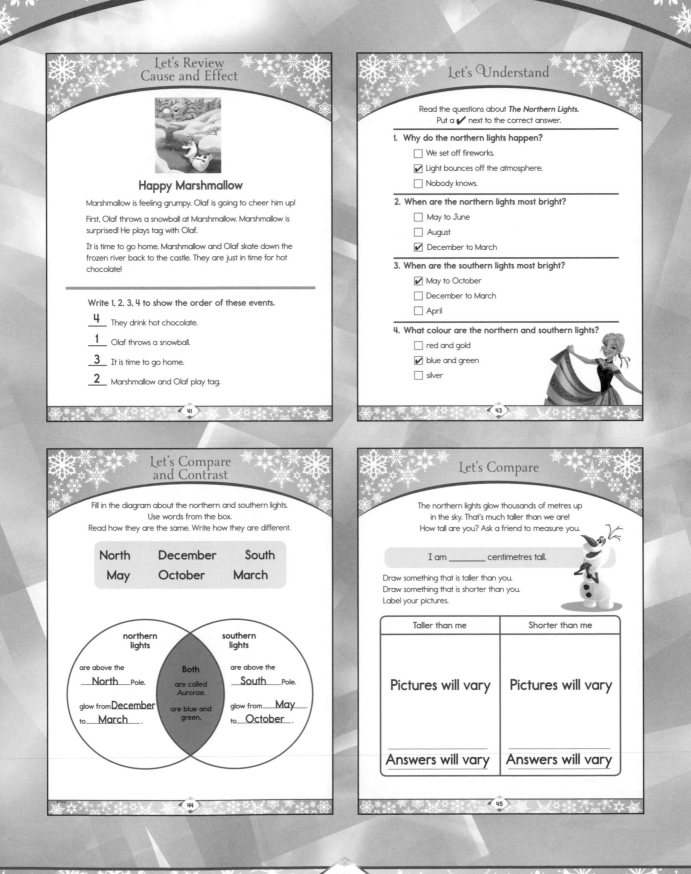

Happy Marshmallow

Marshmallow is feeling grumpy. Olaf is going to cheer him up!

First, Olaf throws a snowball at Marshmallow. Marshmallow is surprised! He plays tag with Olaf.

It is time to go home. Marshmallow and Olaf skate down the frozen river back to the castle. They are just in time for hot chocolate!

Write 1, 2, 3, 4 to show the order of these events.

4   They drink hot chocolate.

1   Olaf throws a snowball.

3   It is time to go home.

2   Marshmallow and Olaf play tag.

41

Let's Understand

Read the questions about *The Northern Lights.*
Put a ✔ next to the correct answer.

1. **Why do the northern lights happen?**
   - ☐ We set off fireworks.
   - ☑ Light bounces off the atmosphere.
   - ☐ Nobody knows.

2. **When are the northern lights most bright?**
   - ☐ May to June
   - ☐ August
   - ☑ December to March

3. **When are the southern lights most bright?**
   - ☑ May to October
   - ☐ December to March
   - ☐ April

4. **What colour are the northern and southern lights?**
   - ☐ red and gold
   - ☑ blue and green
   - ☐ silver

43

Let's Compare
and Contrast

Fill in the diagram about the northern and southern lights.
Use words from the box.
Read how they are the same. Write how they are different.

North	December	South
May	October	March

northern lights

southern lights

are above the **North** Pole.

Both

are called *Aurorae.*

are blue and green.

are above the **South** Pole.

glow from **December** to **March** .

glow from **May** to **October** .

44

Let's Compare

The northern lights glow thousands of metres up in the sky. That's much taller than we are!
How tall are you? Ask a friend to measure you.

I am _____ centimetres tall.

Draw something that is taller than you.
Draw something that is shorter than you.
Label your pictures.

Taller than me	Shorter than me
Pictures will vary	Pictures will vary
Answers will vary	Answers will vary

45

Answers

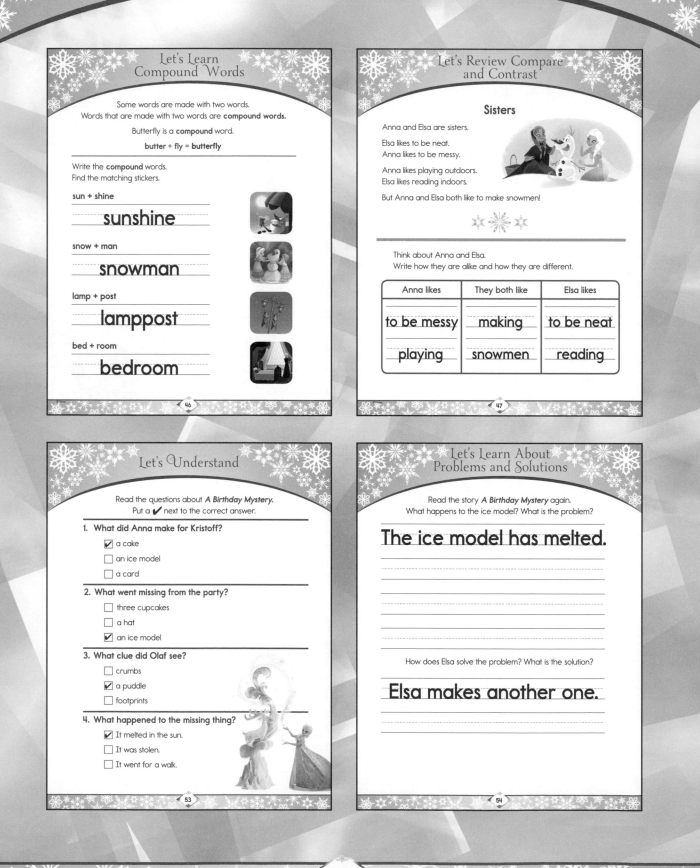

Let's Learn Compound Words

Some words are made with two words.
Words that are made with two words are **compound words**.

Butterfly is a **compound** word.

butter + fly = butterfly

Write the **compound** words.
Find the matching stickers.

sun + shine

sunshine

snow + man

snowman

lamp + post

lamppost

bed + room

bedroom

46

Let's Review Compare and Contrast

Sisters

Anna and Elsa are sisters.

Elsa likes to be neat.
Anna likes to be messy.

Anna likes playing outdoors.
Elsa likes reading indoors.

But Anna and Elsa both like to make snowmen!

Think about Anna and Elsa.
Write how they are alike and how they are different.

Anna likes	They both like	Elsa likes
to be messy	making	to be neat
playing	snowmen	reading

47

Let's Understand

Read the questions about *A Birthday Mystery*.
Put a ✔ next to the correct answer.

1. **What did Anna make for Kristoff?**
   - ✔ a cake
   - ☐ an ice model
   - ☐ a card

2. **What went missing from the party?**
   - ☐ three cupcakes
   - ☐ a hat
   - ✔ an ice model

3. **What clue did Olaf see?**
   - ☐ crumbs
   - ✔ a puddle
   - ☐ footprints

4. **What happened to the missing thing?**
   - ✔ It melted in the sun.
   - ☐ It was stolen.
   - ☐ It went for a walk.

53

Let's Learn About Problems and Solutions

Read the story *A Birthday Mystery* again.
What happens to the ice model? What is the problem?

The ice model has melted.

How does Elsa solve the problem? What is the solution?

Elsa makes another one.

54

72

Answers

Let's Learn Word Meanings

Read each sentence.
Write a word from the box that has the same meaning.
Find the matching sticker.

| race | fun | jump | pretty |

1. This word means *very nice to look at.*

   pretty

2. This word means *to run very fast.*

   race

3. This word means *to have a good time.*

   fun

4. This word means *to spring into the air.*

   jump

Let's Review Problems and Solutions

Read the story, then answer the questions.

The Great Idea

Olaf loved the summertime. He loved to sit on the beach and play in the park. But Olaf was a snowman. A snowman could not stay out in the sun. He would melt if he got too warm!

Elsa had a great idea. She made a small, cold cloud above Olaf's head. It would keep him cool when the day got warm.

Olaf was so happy. He could now spend time in the sunshine!

Put a ✔ next to the correct answer.

1. **What is Olaf's problem?**
   - ☐ He liked the beach.
   - ☑ He would melt if he got too hot.
   - ☐ He didn't do his homework.

2. **How did Elsa solve the problem?**
   - ☑ She created a cold cloud.
   - ☐ She gave Olaf some ice.
   - ☐ She took Olaf to the mountains.

Let's Write

Help write a story about two sisters.
One sister is named Elsa.
Write the name of the other sister.

Anna

There is a reindeer in the story.
What colour is the reindeer?

brown

Write the reindeer's name.

Sven

Now pull out the next page. Fold it to make a book. Fill in the blanks where you see them. Colour the pictures.

Here Are All the Things I Can Do

I can read ...

Fiction ⬤

Non-fiction ⬤

Poems ⬤

Plays ⬤

Put a snowflake sticker next to the things that you can do!

I can ...

Describe characters in a story ⬤

Describe a story's setting ⬤

Describe what happens in the beginning, middle and end of a story ⬤

Answer questions about stories ⬤

Make connections to my own experiences ⬤

Retell stories ⬤

Predict what might happen next in a story ⬤

I can ...

Name story events that cause other things to happen ⚪

Describe how a problem in a story was solved ⚪

Understand how things in a story are alike and different ⚪

I can read ...

Words

skate	race
fun	grins
castle	grabs
snowball	

⚪

Compound words

butterfly	sunshine
snowman	lamppost

⚪

Words with the same meanings

afraid	scared
glad	happy
chilly	cold
angry	mad

⚪

Opposite words

hot	cold
over	under
day	night
happy	sad

⚪

Develop healthy reading habits

To encourage your child to read whenever possible, visit libraries and bookshops together often. Creating a book log can help promote a sense of achievement and keep track of what books your child has read and is currently reading. There are many different kinds of books for you to experience together: silly books, poetry books, information books, picture books, chapter books, craft books and so on. As your child's reading progresses, you will find that they develop their own taste in books that will affect what they choose to read. Daily independent reading time will help nurture your child's healthy reading habits.

Understanding sequences

Your child needs to learn about the sequence of events in both fiction and non-fiction. This helps them to understand a story plot, information or explanations in a non-fiction book. It would help to draw attention to sequences when you complete simple projects or activities. Use words that help to sequence what you are doing, e.g. if you bake a cake, ask:

What do we need to do first?
What do we need to do next?
What do we need to do last?

Talk about books

Talk about the books you read together to extend the reading experience. What were your favourite parts? What did you find funny? What parts were confusing? How did certain characters make you feel? What did different parts of the story remind you of? What happened at the beginning, middle and end of the story. These brief conversations will help your child develop confidence in sharing his or her own questions, opinions and reflections about a story or book.

Predicting what will happen

If your child has had many different types of reading experiences then they will be better equipped to be able to predict what happens in a story. If they can make predictions they can relate this story to their own experience which will help their understanding. Prediction can also help to focus them on their reading and also to make them excited about what might happen next. When you child is reading to you, stop them and ask them what they think might happen next to the character/s at that point of the story.

Make up new endings

After reading a favourite story together, talk about ways to change the ending. What would happen if the character did something differently? What would happen if a new character came along? What would happen if you changed how the story problem was solved?

Relating to own experiences

When talking about the book your child has read or you have read to your child, encourage them to compare aspects with their own lives. Are they like the character? Is the setting like where they live? Have they gone through the same experience as the character?

Finding new words

Stop your child when they are reading to you and ask them if they know the meaning of the word they have read. Discuss whether the word is an opposite word or whether it is a word that has the same meaning as another word. Use dictionaries to find out about the meaning of words. Ask your child why they think that particular word has been used and whether other words could have been used instead.

CONGRATULATIONS!

_____

(Name)

has completed the Disney Learning Workbook:

READING AND COMPREHENSION

Presented on

_____

(Date)

_____

(Parent's Signature)

From the movie
Disney
FROZEN

© Disney

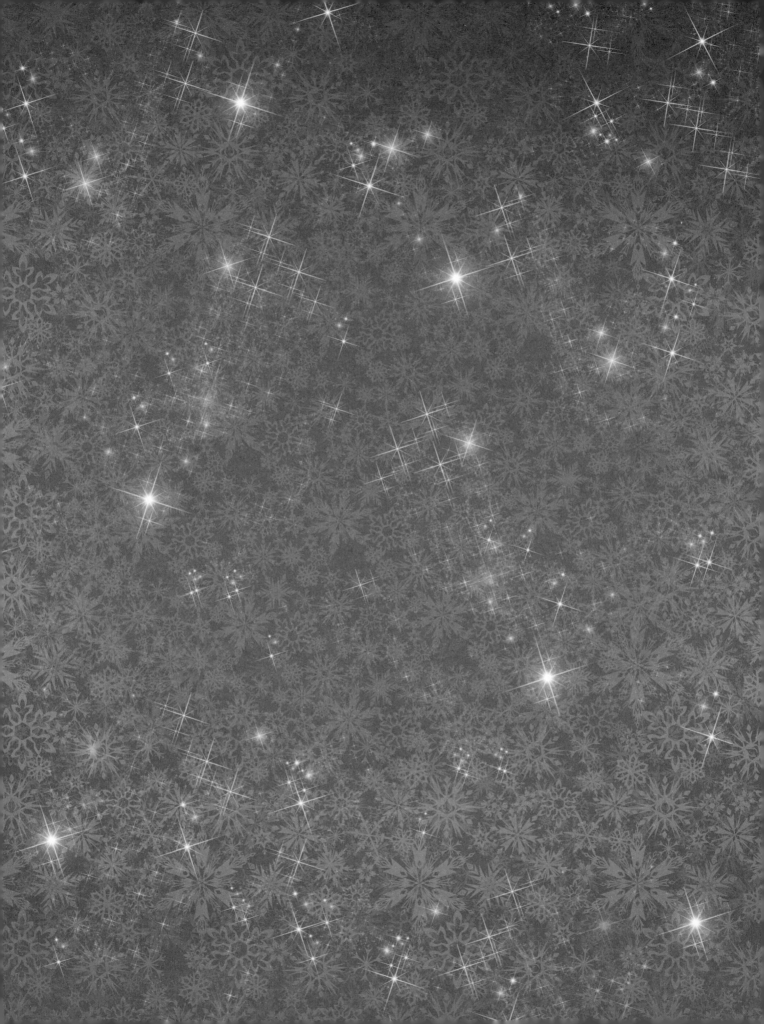